Sixteen Letters

Aradhana Thakor

Copyright © 2020 Aradhana Thakor

All rights reserved

No part of this book may be reproduced, or stored in a retrieval system, or transmitted in any form or by any means, electronic, mechanical, photocopying, recording, or otherwise, without express written permission of the author. Scripture quotations taken from The Holy Bible, New International Version (NIV).

ISBN- 9798561306952

Contents

Title Page
Copyright
Introduction — 1
Letter #1 Choicest Arrow — 4
Letter #2 Limitless God — 6
Letter #3 You Are Worthy — 8
Letter #4 Shout Victory! — 10
Letter #5 I See You — 12
Letter #6 Redeemed — 15
Letter #7 Why Lord Why? — 17
Letter #8 How Could You Lord? — 21
Letter #9 Breaking Point — 24
Letter #10 Move Onward My Soul — 26
Letter #11 My Healer — 29
Letter #12 At His Feet — 31
Letter #13 Suffer For Christ — 33

Letter #14 Great High Priest	36
Letter #15 Carry Others	39
Letter #16 Adopted	42
Acknowledgement	45
Books By This Author	47

Introduction

Dear traveler in Christ,

A long round of applause to you for journeying this far in the truth of our Lord Jesus Christ and who continues steadfastly on this road with the eternal hope to see Him face to face. The road to Calvary is indeed a hard one with its steep craggy slopes, lofty peaks, winding pathways, and deep valleys. Living by faith is not easy; it was not for Jesus either. "We must go through many hardships to enter the kingdom of God." (Acts 14:22 NIV).

This book is an answer to prayer. One day I sought the Lord and asked Him to reveal to me exactly what He wanted me to write. Here is the seed that He planted in my heart:

"My child, I want you to offer a cool refreshing

drink to all my weary travelers that will quench their parched throats, strengthen their weak knees, provide renewed vigor so they may take hold of my promises with a new grip and soar on wings like eagles. Be a cool oasis so they can rest, reflect, and rejuvenate as they journey towards me. Encourage each other in love while you are here on earth and thereby have a global harmony of souls and kindred spirits in Christ."

And so, here are my 16 letters to you. Each letter has been tried, tested, and sealed by our Lord. They have been my "manna" which I received while journeying on this road till date and I hope they provide nourishment to you as you journey on. After reading my 16 letters, I encourage you to write down your 16 letters (or even more as the Lord leads you) to pass onto another fellow traveler who needs a refreshing drink and thereby carry each other across the finish line.

Note: You do not have to write a book to do this. I am sure your Bible contains these little markings or notes that you have made of verses that deeply comfort you and you keep going back to them as they speak to your heart every single time. Just write down these verses and explain briefly how they have nourished your spirit. Then simply hand these letters to someone you know who is journeying on this road and encourage them to write down their letters to pass onto another fellow traveler. You may not know just how precious your letters might be to someone who is on the verge of falling off the cliff and desperately needs a lifeline.

Letter #1 Choicest Arrow

Before I was born the Lord called me; from my mother's womb he has spoken my name. He made my mouth like a sharpened sword, in the shadow of his hand he hid me; he made me into a polished arrow and concealed me in his quiver. (Isaiah 49:1-2 NIV).

Our Dear Lord had His eyes on you before you were even conceived. Up to this present moment, He has been carefully sharpening, polishing, and chiseling you so He can use you at just the right moment. A quiver is traditionally a container, or a bag made of leather or fur. An archer ties it securely on his back. He conceals only the choicest arrows this close to him so he can draw them swiftly when he sees the enemy approaching. The Lord sees you as his choicest arrow which He will draw in His time. Be of good cheer those of you who long to do something for Christ. Believe that you are now in His quiver ready to be summoned at any time. What a privilege to be enlisted in His army!

The enemy is quickly closing in on me
I hear angry hooves gallop towards me
Swiftly my archer reaches for his quiver
Draws on me with hands that don't shiver
With skilled fingers he stretches his bow
And aims accurately and lets me go
I strike the advancing enemy to the ground
And rejoice to see my archer safe and sound

Letter #2 Limitless God

Open wide your mouth and I will fill it. (Psalm 81:10 NIV).

In 1835, a young George Mueller made a bargain with God and staked all his dreams on this promise, "Open wide your mouth and I will fill it." He had a dream to build an orphanage in Bristol, England. He struck a deal with God that he would only look upon him to provide all the finances and would not ask any man for help. What holy audacity! By the end of 1870, he had built five orphanages, was providing for 2000 orphans, and was doing it all by prayer and faith. In all those years he never asked anyone for even a shilling! Oh, is there any limit to what our God can do? Only childlike faith and obedience to His will is needed on our part. If you are in line with His will then He is just waiting for you to open your heart in faith so, He can lavishly fill it until it overflows.

∞∞∞

My child, I hold the universe in my hand
So, ask me anything for I am at your command
Open your heart wide so I can fill it
I don't want you to place any limit
Then let your faith soar high
As you obey my word and come nigh
To receive my gifts as they lovingly flow
Then shall your cup begin to overflow

Letter #3 You Are Worthy

The world was not worthy of them.
(Hebrews 11:38 NIV).

The early Christians had to face a lot of persecution for the sake of the Gospel. Some were tortured, flogged, mistreated, chained, and even stoned to death. Others were sawed in half and some killed by the sword. By the world's standard they were an utter failure on earth. But in our Lord's eyes, they were too good for this world. In fact, the world was not worthy of them! The world failed to recognize their worth.

Has the world made you feel insignificant and unworthy? Then look up to these bright examples before you and carry on your journey towards Him who understands your worth.

∞∞∞

Though the world belittles me
And wants nothing to do with me
Though they think my life is a waste
And they judge me in such a haste
Though they think am a failure on earth
I smile because My Savior knows my worth

Letter #4 Shout Victory!

"It is finished." (John 19:30 NIV).

Everyone thought Jesus' life had tragically ended and it appeared to His disciples that He failed to carry out His mission. To His enemies it appeared that they had finally conquered their most dangerous Enemy. By all appearances it seemed that His life had come to a tragic end. Just then the triumphant cry of victory was shouted out, "It is finished." These three words shout victory! This was the shout of victory in the darkest hour.

If you feel like all your efforts have failed, everything points to despair and the enemy has gained ascendency, you can also shout victory. This is real victory, to shout triumphantly in Christ though all around is darkness. So next time you feel despondent, look up to Christ and claim victory because He has overcome the world.

∞∞∞

No matter what may be your story
Remember that He shouted victory
You too can shout victory in the darkest hour
Coz to Him, this is the highest form of honor

Letter #5 I See You

What is mankind that you are mindful of them, human beings that you care for them? (Psalm 8:4 NIV).

A few years ago, I had the privilege to board Costa Deliziosa, an Italian cruise liner, courtesy of my husband who was, at that time, the Executive Sous Chef for this vessel. She was a beauty clothed in the finest white that stretched 964 feet 7 inches and had the capacity to carry 4000 passengers and crew.

One morning when we reached the local port, I was shocked to see a bunch of tiny objects floating on the water. Upon a closer look I realized that they were local fishermen boats. They seemed so fragile and helpless in the face of this monstrosity of a vessel. Just then the realization hit me that this is how I must appear to our Lord when He looks down from heaven at me. This miniscule fragile life which the Bible compares to the grass, which is new in the morning, withers by evening, gets tossed by the wind and is here today and gone tomorrow is so highly valued by Him. Our little worries and fretting about tomorrow must seem so pointless to Him.

Let us honor Him by thanking Him for this little breath in our nostrils which He has graciously bestowed on us. No matter how microscopic you might seem in His eyes He cares about you for He has numbered every single hair on your head and encompasses you with His love every minute and every second of every day. Take courage, little one; He has His eye on you!

Have you heard of this story?
About the Grass and the Oak tree
One day the Oak in all its splendor
Looks down on the Grass so tender,
Questions the Grass, "I wonder
why God created you,

You're tossed by the wind and of no use"
The Grass gazes lovingly towards the blue sky
And says, "I am content and dare not ask Him why,
For am sure I must bring Him some pleasure,
When He sees me dancing in the wind
sent from His house of treasure."

Letter #6 Redeemed

I consider that our present sufferings are not worth comparing with the glory that will be revealed in us. (Romans 8:18 NIV).

While journeying on this road have you ever wondered about that forsaken career, oppositions, misunderstandings, constant struggles, unanswered prayers, delays, hard-fought battles, conflicts with the enemy, ridicule from peers, hours of intercession, midnight pleadings with God, bereavements, being worn out in His service, battered in health, loss of all earthly honor, deep soul anguish, and thought, "Is it all really worth it?"

Then I point you to that multitude of redeemed souls singing Glory Hallelujah with the heavenly hosts worshiping at His throne. What glory, what joy awaits us in heaven! We get to see our Dear Lord face to face. We will worship at His throne day and night. He who sits on the throne will shelter us with His presence. Never again will there be hunger or thirst. The Lamb will be our shepherd who will lead us to springs of living water. He will wipe every tear from our eyes. (Revelations 7:15-17 NIV). There will be no more death or mourning or crying or pain. (Revelations 21:4 NIV). We will reunite with our loved ones. We will be His for all eternity. We will reign with Him forever.

Heaven rejoices when one soul is won
Someday we shall see a glorious sun
When all humanity bows down
Then shall heaven echo songs from souls won

Letter #7 Why Lord Why?

Can you pull in Leviathan with a fishhook or tie down its tongue with a rope? (Job 41:1 NIV).

At some point in our life we find ourselves in the same position as Job. Our world seems to crumble around us. Nothing seems to make any sense. God seems distant and silent to our cries. Like Job we go through emotional cycles. We whine, doubt, explode, collapse and wallow in self-pity. We begin to question God and His existence. Job wanted answers from God. He wanted God to appear to him so He could explain his miserable condition. When God finally speaks, Job was not prepared for what He had to say.

God talks about the wonders of the natural world He created. He points out one by one, His works of creation of which He is proud. He talks about the magnificent display of natural phenomena – solar systems, constellations, thunderstorms. He then talks about the strength and beauty of wild animals which He created. He explains in detail about one of His sea creatures the, "Leviathan". The Leviathan is believed to have some features of a crocodile and some as a dragon. In other places the Bible refers to it as either a whale-like creature (Psalm 104:26 NIV) or a serpent or monster of the sea (Isaiah 27:1 NIV). It is pictured as being incredibly powerful and uncontrollable.

Job finally gets the message: If you cannot attempt to take on God's powerful creatures, then do not attempt to question its creator. God does not need Job or anyone else to tell Him how to run the world. God even asks Job, "Would you like to run the universe for a while? Go ahead, try designing an ostrich, a mountain goat or even a snowflake." If you cannot understand the visible things of this world, how do you expect to understand the world you cannot even see? In the end, we see that everything worked out well for Job and God blessed the latter part of his life more than the former. Let us not question His method and ways, dear one. God is in control of every aspect of your life. He knows what He is doing. Just trust and rely on His faithfulness.

∞∞∞

Why, Lord, Why?
Lord, I don't understand your way
I come before You as my strength gives away
My world seems to crumble around me
All my dreams and hopes lay shattered before me
Why, Lord, Why?

Why did you make me see this awful day
When all I wanted was to follow your way
You could have prevented this from coming
Can't you see, it's left my heart fuming?
Why, Lord, Why?

Oh! Beloved, before I formed you in the womb I knew you
I always knew the plans I had designed for you

Did you forget, I am the potter and you the clay?

*Did you forget while creating you,
you didn't have a say?*

*Did you forget that I will never
leave you nor forsake you?*

*Or did you forget that I cause all things
to work together for your good too?*

My Child, you can trust the man that died for you

Christ who paid the heavy price for you

Shed every drop for your salvation and peace

*So that all your anxious thoughts
about this earthly life may cease*

So, even when you do not understand my way

*You can trust the man that died
for you is all I will say*

So, here's my final question to you

Will you trust the man that died for you?

Letter #8 How Could You Lord?

"Abraham believed God and it was credited to him as righteousness. Now to the one who works, wages is not credited as a gift but as an obligation. However, to the one who does not work but trusts God who justifies the ungodly, their faith is credited as righteousness." (Romans 4:3-5 NIV).

Could we ever fathom just how loving and compassionate our God truly is?

It blows my mind when I think of the great divine plan of God in sending his only Son to bring about justification and righteousness for us. I love to read the book of Romans which tells me what an undeserving sinner I am and how much he loved me to send his only Son to die for my sins when I didn't even know Him. Not just that, but how freely he has given me the gift of righteousness and made peace with me. Because of our faith in Christ, we now have the abundant provision of grace in which we now stand. What marvelous truths and hidden treasures God has revealed to us through his Word. And who does He reveal it to? He reveals it to us, undeserving sinners. Oh! If only we could grasp "how wide and long and high and deep is the love of Christ in forgiving us sinners! Though your sins are like scarlet, they shall be as white as snow; though they are red as crimson, they shall be like wool. (Isaiah 1:18). This is the free gift of forgiveness available to all repenting sinners. You have a gracious loving Father in heaven that understands you and has only your best interests at heart because you are the apple of His eye.

How could you Lord
Love someone like me?
When I was the one to turn by back on thee

How could you Lord
Shed every drop of your blood for me?
When I was the one to curse thee
How could you Lord
Give me the free gift of eternal life?
When I never bothered to look up to you in my strife
How could you Lord
Wash all my sins away?
When I was the one that kept running away
How could you Lord
Forgive a sinner like me?
When I was lost in my sins and
never thought of thee
How could you Lord
How could you?
My Child, my divine love for you was so deep
That my own precious Son I didn't keep
Made Him the Sacrificial Lamb
So that you may finally know who I am

Letter #9 Breaking Point

We are hard pressed on every side, but not crushed; perplexed, but not in despair; persecuted, but not abandoned; struck down, but not destroyed. (2 Corinthians 4:8-9 NIV).

There have been times when I felt that I have reached my wits end, my breaking point. This verse has always comforted and given me new vigor to continue my journey. You may find yourself surrounded by trouble on all sides, yet He sustains us, so we don't give up. You may find yourself confused by situations, yet He surrounds us with songs of deliverance, so we don't give in to self pity. You may yet be tortured by the enemy; He does not leave your side. You may even find yourself being overtaken, beaten, and conquered by the enemy yet He keeps you from being destroyed in Spirit by bestowing on us His divine grace and strength.

Your way is too hard I cried
Lord, give me a burden light
My child! I know your might
Thy way before you, I have tried

Letter #10 Move Onward My Soul

My God, my God, why have you forsaken me? Why are you so far from saving me, so far from my cries of anguish? (Psalm 22:1 NIV).

For every emotion or mood, you can find a psalm to match. Most of the psalms are credited to King David. What I love the most is the fact that King David wrestled with all kinds of human emotions and experiences while living the life of faith. At times, he cried to God in deep anguish of soul, "How long, Lord, how long? I am worn out from my groaning." At times he questioned Him about his suffering. Frequently he asked, "Where are you, God? Why don't you help me?" At times he broke out into a spontaneous song of deliverance when the

Lord rescues him. At times he was overcome with anger and guilt for he is sneered and mocked by his enemies who plot violence against him. For the psalmist, faith in God was a struggle yet he had a deep conviction that God would overcome his enemies. He believed that God was his fortress, strength, and joy. We can see that even the best men like David; the great king suffered agony and felt abandoned.

Move onward my soul
For this is your goal

Even though I see Him not
As my enemy plans a violent plot
I will still trust in You
As my heart waits for your rescue

Move onward my soul
For this is your goal

Doubt not in His power

In His time He will answer
His mighty arm He will raise
And fill you with His song of praise

Move onward my soul
For this is my goal

Letter #11 My Healer

I will bring health and healing to it; I will heal my people and will let them enjoy abundant peace and security. (Jeremiah 33:6 NIV).

I have grasped and clenched at this verse very tightly during times of sickness. Over the years I have learnt that healing can come instantly and at times we may have to endure it through delays, but His grace keeps us from getting discouraged and eventually he brings about our healing. He also taught me that there may also be times He may not take it completely away but rather provides us a way to cheerfully endure it and makes us a blessing to others while on your sickbed.

The Lord also taught me that He can bring healing to my heart as well. We often carry scars and bruises in our heart. Sometimes words have the power to pierce the heart and leave it wounded for years. An unkind gesture, stinging words or an unpleasant memory can leave you emotionally wounded. You may have forgiven the person that hurt you, but an invisible wall which needs to be broken down still exists between you and the person who wounded you. Only Jesus can break down those walls. It's only our Loving Father that can bring healing to your body, broken relations, family ties or even marriage. He is only waiting for you to call on Him.

As I offer my life
In His hands to heal
He lovingly takes it
And marks it with His seal

Letter #12 At His Feet

And provide for those who grieve in Zion – to bestow on them a crown of beauty instead of ashes, the oil of joy instead of mourning, and a garment of praise instead of a spirit of despair. (Isaiah 61:3 NIV).

Our Lord is calling you to come to this anointed place of exchange which is at Jesus' feet. Whenever you feel your work has amounted to nothing, when you look around and everything seems to have failed, you can seek Him in prayer and there at His feet you can replace your ashes for His beauty. He has a never-ending supply of that precious oil of joy which can be applied to every hurt and sorrow. There at His feet you can replace your spirit of despair for His spirit of praise and thereby be refreshed by His anointed dewdrops from heaven. After you gain nourishment at His feet, He will establish you firmly like an Oak so you can display His splendor to the world.

Let me tell you a secret,
Of a paradise I have found
To replace all my burdens
Whenever I am feeling down
I carry all my worries as I go
Only to return with an anointed glow
Let me tell you a secret,
Of this most sacred seat
I found it there when I abide
At His precious feet

Letter #13 Suffer For Christ

Dear friends, do not be surprised at the fiery ordeal that has come on you to test you, as though something strange were happening to you. But rejoice inasmuch as you participate in the sufferings of Christ, so that you may be overjoyed when his glory is revealed. (1 Peter 4:12-13 NIV).

There have been countless religion-inspired bloodbaths throughout history. Twentieth century has seen the tragic massacre of millions of Christian Armenians by Turkish forces. Thousands of Christians died in Africa during Ugandan dictator Idi Amin's reign of terror. Countless Christians suffered under the Soviet, Chinese and Indian governments, and the oppression continues. Today persecution of Christians around the globe has reached a near "genocide" level.

My dear traveler, don't let suffering catch you

off guard. It is an expected and vital part of your journey. You will have to pass through the valley of the shadow of death to feel His protection and presence.

Oh! What a privilege to suffer for Christ! It is a way to participate in His glory. It gives Him great pleasure when you suffer cheerfully without staggering in faith for His sake. The Bible says, "If you are insulted because of the name of Christ, you are blessed, for the Spirit of glory and of God rests on you." (1 Peter 4:14 NIV). If you suffer for being a Christian; rejoice and praise Him that you bear that name. Do not be ashamed but instead feel honored to share in His sufferings and remember that all your fellow travelers are going through the same ordeal. Your enemy the devil prowls around like a roaring lion looking for someone to devour. Resist him, standing firm in the faith, because you know that the family of believers throughout the world is undergoing the same kind of sufferings. (1 Peter 5:8-9 NIV).

What is your greatest gain?
If you had a chance to ask this,
Am sure the apostle Paul
Would answer something like this,
"I still see Christ's heart bleed,
For the countless lost souls in need,
To share His great burning pain,
In this I see my greatest gain."

Letter #14 Great High Priest

Therefore he is able to save completely those who come to God through him, because he always lives to intercede for them. (Hebrews 7:25 NIV).

Not only did He bear the sins of the entire world, but He conquered death and is now seated at the right hand of God. His work did not end here. God designated Him to be a great high priest who ever lives to intercede "for" you. In the Old Testament, only the high priest could enter the Most Holy Place where he would offer sacrifices for his sins and the sins of the people. But now Jesus has already entered that inner sanctuary behind the curtain on our behalf where he intercedes for you.

For Christ did not enter a sanctuary made with human hands that was only a copy of the true one; he entered heaven itself, now to appear for us in God's presence. (Hebrews 9:24 NIV). He is the perfect high priest who knows your weaknesses and intercedes for you before the throne of God, so you don't give up. Sometimes God permits your life to be shaken by storm after storm. Your life seems devastated, uprooted, and laid bare. Your faith seems to wobble. Your grasp on His promises slowly begins to slip. You don't know what to pray for. What should you do?

Just be still and know that He is God. Our loving God even made intercession for his transgressors while he was being tortured. (Isaiah 53:12 NIV).

The Spirit helps us in our weakness. We do not know what we ought to pray for, but the Spirit himself intercedes for us through wordless groans. And he who searches our hearts knows the mind of the Spirit, because the Spirit intercedes for God's people in accordance with the will of God. (Romans 8:26-27 NIV).

Our Loving Father in heaven will not let you

stumble and fall but will uphold you in your faith till the end. Christ, himself is interceding for you before the throne of God so you can stand firm till the end and receive your eternal inheritance.

When prayer becomes an effort for me
And my soul cannot find Him close
I rejoice coz The Almighty God knows
When my Great High Priest intercedes for me

Letter #15 Carry Others

Carry each other's burdens, and in this way you will fulfill the law of Christ. (Galatians 6:2 NIV).

During this upward climb you may come across a fellow climber who might need to take hold of your hand in order to balance their grip on these craggy hills. Let us not judge or question their endurance level but rather uphold them in prayer and supplication.

John Hyde was one of the main leaders present at the Sailkot Convention of 1906 in India. A brother writes about this Convention and the agony of soul which was reflected in them regarding one daughter in Christ. This excerpt is taken from the book, "Challenge to Prayer."

"An Indian Christian girl was at this Convention. Her father had compelled her to neglect Christ's claims upon her. In the prayer room she was convicted of her sin, and told how her heart was being torn away from her father to Christ. One could almost see the springing tendrils of her heart as the power of the love of Christ came upon her. It was a terrible time. Then she asked us to pray for her father. We began to pray, and suddenly the great burden of that soul was cast upon us, and the room was filled with sobs and cries for one whom most of us had never seen or heard of before. Strong men lay on the ground groaning in agony for that soul. There was not a dry eye in that place until at last God have us the assurance that prayer had been heard and out of Gethsemane we came into the Pentecostal joy of being able to praise Him that He heard our cry."

No doubt it is a steep climb
But it is your divine duty to shine
Light for a weary wandering soul
So that they too can cross the finish line

Letter #16 Adopted

In love he predestined us for adoption to sonship through Jesus Christ, in accordance with his pleasure and will. (Ephesians 1:5 NIV).

What a glorious honor to be adopted by God! There is no need to feel depressed if you don't have any earthly riches or inheritance to claim. Look at the marvelous riches which you have already inherited in Christ. Christians have been adopted directly into the family of God. In him you have inherited redemption through the blood of Christ, the forgiveness of sins according to the riches of God's grace that he lavished on us. (Ephesians 1:7 NIV). According to the apostle Paul, you have been branded with a seal which is the ultimate mark of ownership. The Holy Spirit is a "deposit" guaranteeing a great inheritance. (Ephesians 1:13-14 NIV). You have also inherited God's incomparably great power and strength which He exerted when He raised Christ from the dead and seated him at his right hand in the heavenly realms. (Ephesians 1:19-20 NIV). You are no longer foreigners and strangers but fellow citizens with God's people and also members of his household. (Ephesians 2:19 NIV).

I have no earthly wealth I confess
But an everlasting treasure I do possess
This eternal truth to which I cling,
"I have been adopted by the King of Kings!"

Acknowledgement

All praise and honor to my Lord and Savior Jesus Christ for using me for His kingdom and glory. This book had to endure many obstacles to get to you. There was a period when I was unable to do the thing I love the most, that is to write. I thought my writing days were over and that this book would never see the light of day but He is a compassionate God who graciously bestowed His unending supply of strength to me in order to complete what He started.

A special thanks to my husband, Anoop, for his incredible support and loving me through it all. Anoop, you never cease to amaze me.

Helen Khan, author of, "Shrouds over Eden," a beautiful woman with the kindest heart who has done the difficult task of editing this book, thank you for all your help.

My pray while writing this book and before publishing has been that it falls into the hands of those who need it the most so the Holy Spirit can whisper in their hearts.

Books By This Author

Burning Passion For Lost Souls

This book takes you on a thrilling and emotional journey of one man's burning passion for lost souls behind bars. This beautiful journey is seen through the eyes of a daughter which she narrates in the form of poetry that uplifts and warms your soul. As you go on this journey, you will also experience the unfailing and everlasting love of Christ which is revealed in the life-changing testimonies of prisoners. May you be blessed as you journey on…

Made in the USA
Columbia, SC
14 November 2020